A Day in the Life: Desert Animals

Bactrian Camel

Anita Ganeri

Heinemann
LIBRARY

Chicago, Illinois

www.heinemannraintree.com
Visit our website to find out
more information about
Heinemann-Raintree books.

To order:
☎ Phone 888-454-2279
💻 Visit www.heinemannraintree.com
to browse our catalog and order online.

Edited by Daniel Nunn, Rebecca Rissman, and Sian Smith
Designed by Richard Parker
Picture research by Elizabeth Alexander
Production by Victoria Fitzgerald
Originated by Capstone Global Library Ltd
Printed and bound in China by South China Printing
 Company Ltd

14 13 12 11 10
10 9 8 7 6 5 4 3 2 1

**Library of Congress Cataloging-in-
Publication Data**
Ganeri, Anita, 1961–
 Bactrian camel / Anita Ganeri.
  p. cm. — (A day in the life. Desert animals)
 Includes bibliographical references and index.
 ISBN 978-1-4329-4770-5 (hc)
 ISBN 978-1-4329-4779-8 (pb)
 1. Bactrian camel—Juvenile literature. I.Title.
 QL737.U54G357 2011
 599.63'62—dc22   2010022818

Acknowledgments

We would like to thank the following for permission to
reproduce photographs: Alamy p. 18 (© Vic Pigula),
Corbis pp. 4 (© Tuul/Hemis), 5, 23 glossary desert, 23
glossary dromedary (© photocake.de/plainpicture), 14
(© Guo Jian She/Redlink), 20 (© Frans Lanting); FLPA pp.
10, 23 glossary herd (ImageBroker), 11 (Colin Monteath/
Minden Pictures); Getty Images pp. 15 (Peter DeMarco),
17, 23 glossary mammal (Art Wolfe/The Image Bank);
iStockphoto pp. 12, 23 glossary energy (© Anna Yu), 22,
23 glossary hump (© David Kerkhoff), 23 glossary fat (©
Jolanta Dabrowska); Photolibrary pp. 8 (Bruno Morandi/
age fotostock), 9, 23 glossary nostrils (Juniors Bildarchiv),
16 (Konstantin Mikhailov/Russian Look), 19 (Guido
Alberto Rossi/Tips Italia), 21 (E.R. DEGGINGER/Animals
Animals); Shutterstock pp. 7, 13 (© Pichugin Dmitry).
Front cover photograph of a Bactrian camel reproduced
with permission of Corbis © Theo Allofs.

Back cover photograph of (left) a Bactrian camel eating
(Camelus bactrianus domesticus) reproduced with
permission of iStockphoto (© Anna Yu); and (right) a
Bactrian camel in the Mongolian Desert reproduced with
permission of Shutterstock (© Pichugin Dmitry).

We would like to thank Michael Bright for his assistance in
the preparation of this book.

Contents

Some words are shown in bold, **like this**.
You can find them in the glossary on page 23.

What Is a Bactrian Camel?

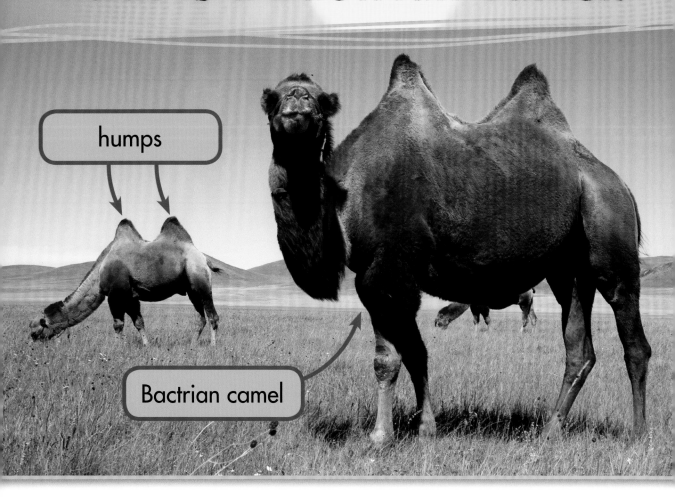

humps

Bactrian camel

A camel is a **mammal**.

All mammals have some hair on their bodies and feed their babies milk.

hump

dromedary

Camels that only have one **hump** are called **dromedaries** or Arabian camels.

This book is about Bactrian camels, which have two humps.

Where Do Bactrian Camels Live?

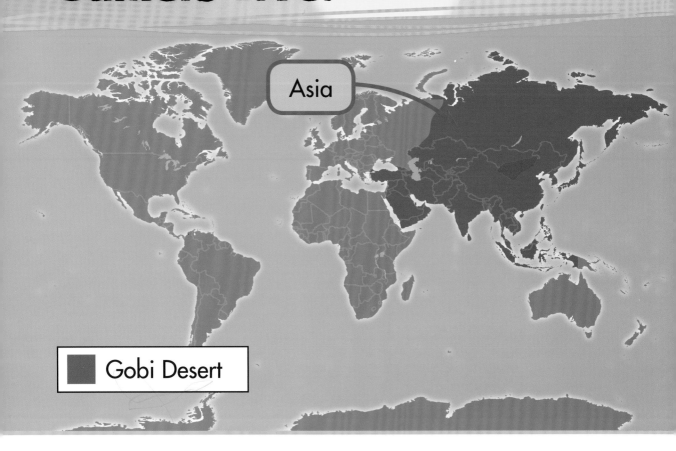

Asia

Gobi Desert

Bactrian camels live in the Gobi **Desert** in Asia.

Can you find this desert on the map?

The desert is hot in the summer but cold in winter, with very little rain.

Most of the desert is rocky and stony, with some sand.

What Do Bactrian Camels Look Like?

coat

Bactrian camels are large, with long necks, long legs, and two big **humps**.

Their brown coats grow thicker in winter to keep them warm.

eyelashes

nostril

A Bactrian camel has thick eyelashes for keeping dust and sand out of its eyes.

It can also close its **nostrils** to stop sand and dust from getting in.

What Do Bactrian Camels Do During the Day?

Bactrian camels look for food in the morning.

They walk long distances to find food and water.

The camels have tough feet for walking on rocky ground.

They can also spread their toes out wide for walking on soft, sandy ground.

What Do Bactrian Camels Eat?

Bactrian camels mostly eat **desert** plants that they find during the day.

They have tough mouths and can even eat prickly or thorny plants.

A camel's **hump** is a store of **fat**.

The camels use the fat to give them **energy** when they cannot find food to eat.

Do Bactrian Camels Need to Drink?

Bactrian camels can go for days without drinking water.

This is useful in the **desert**, where there is not much water.

If the camels find some water, they can drink about six bucketfuls at a time.

They also get water from the plants they eat.

Do Bactrian Camels Live in Groups?

Bactrian camels live in family groups, called **herds**.

There are usually about six camels in a herd, but sometimes more.

Baby camels are born in spring.

A baby stays in the herd with its mother until it is about three years old.

Do Bactrian Camels Have Any Enemies?

People have hunted wild Bactrian camels for a long time.

There are not many wild Bactrian camels left.

Some people use Bactrian camels and keep them safe.

Bactrian camels can help people to carry things across the **desert**.

What Do Bactrian Camels Do at Night?

At night, the camels go to sleep on the ground.

Their thick fur keeps them warm.

The camels sleep with their legs tucked under their bodies.

They hold their heads high up in the air.

Bactrian Camel Body Map

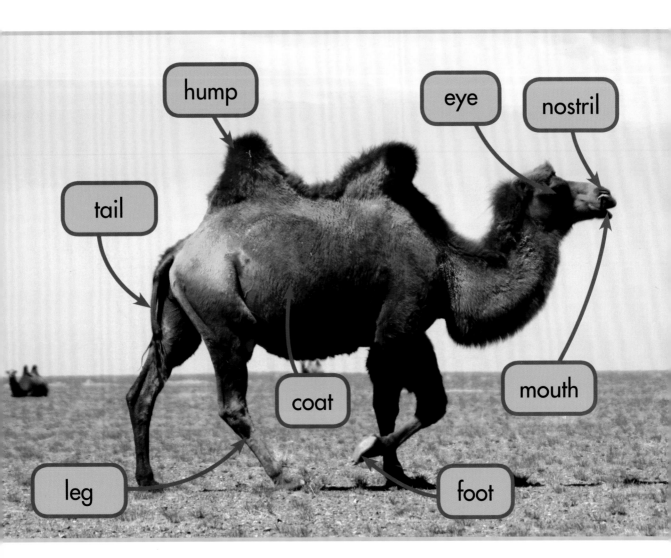

hump

eye

nostril

tail

coat

mouth

leg

foot

Glossary

 **desert** very dry place that is rocky, stony, or sandy

 **dromedary** camel with one hump. Dromedaries are also called Arabian camels.

 **energy** power to do something

 **fat** oily thing in some foods. Animals use fat in their bodies to give them energy.

 **herd** family group of camels

 **hump** store of fat on a camel's back

 **mammal** animal that feeds its babies milk. All mammals have some hair or fur on their bodies.

 **nostrils** openings around a camel's nose

Find Out More

Books

Haldane, Elizabeth. *Desert: Around the Clock with the Animals of the Desert* (24 Hours). New York: Dorling Kindersley, 2006.

Hodge, Deborah. *Desert Animals* (Who Lives Here?). Toronto: Kids Can Press, 2008.

MacAulay, Kelley, and Bobbie Kalman. *Desert Habitat* (Introducing Habitats). New York: Crabtree, 2008.

Websites

Learn more about Bactrian camels at: **http://kids.nationalgeographic. com/kids/animals/creaturefeature/camels**

Learn more interesting facts about Bactrian camels at: **www.stlzoo.org/ animals/abouttheanimals/mammals/hoofedmammals/bactriancamel.htm**

Index